PRAISE FOR AHARON SHABTAI

"Aharon Shabtai's elegaic poems are all heart in Peter Cole's magnificent translation. This is a poetry of the fragility of old age; a poetry of sorrow for a country whose peace he won't live to see; a poetry that serves Memory, the mother of the Muses. As a renowned translator of ancient Greek poetry into modern Hebrew, Shabtai has the epigrammatic touch, that way of chiseling lines so that the words ring in the memory. His long 'Requiem,' which specifies the dead by their names and an illuminating anecdotal detail, should remind us all that the smallest particulars of a man or woman's life are worth more in God's ledger than any windy abstraction uttered by pundits, celebrities, activists, and politicians: 'Before I fall asleep // Grandpa Beier / undresses // and leaves / on the floor // a large, / clumsy hernia belt // like /a horse's harness.'"
  —Ange Mlinko

"Amidst the rubble, the haunted memories, the vengeful, the corrupt and the power-mad, in short, in the tragic maelstrom of this moment, how to mourn, what to celebrate, how to give voice both to the innocent victims of war and the 'disciples of peace'? How affirm a shared humanity beyond the limits of religious, ideological and territorial claims? These are among the fraught questions renowned Israeli poet Aharon Shabtai raises in this moving late collection, skillfully translated by Peter Cole."
  —Michael Palmer

"Stylistically and intellectually Shabtai is a poet of the first rank."
  —*Antioch Review*

"Aharon Shabtai's *J'accuse*, a slim volume in the prophetic vein, packs a terrific wallop. His skillful fusion of political and aesthetic concerns garners a disorienting, unhinging (because unseemly) erotic charge for his subject matter and revivifies issues closed for too long in dead language. He is a wild man: it is as if he has tried, and failed, to inoculate himself by swallowing a dose of the region's madness."
  —Jonathan Wilson, *The New York Times Book Review*

"Aharon Shabtai's poetry is of epic range: personal and historical, full of hard-won knowledge and the sexual dramas the Greeks allowed their gods and themselves. He can be placed in a line that stretches from biblical and Greek origins to Catullus to Joyce to Jean Genet and other masters of language, revelry, and revelation."
  —Stanley Moss

"Desperate times call for desperate measures. The Hebrew poet Aharon Shabtai, an erudite classicist and literary troublemaker, has written a shocking book of poems that is powered by political rage against the Israeli government. The very title of the volume itself, *J'accuse*, is terrifically charged. It is not for the fainthearted. I find it an upsetting and provocative book. In his excellent introduction, the translator, Peter Cole, compares Shabtai to the classical figure of Archilochus the Scold. He points out that Shabtai moves with disturbing ease between the poles of praise and scorn, lyric flights and biological matter-of-factness."
  —Edward Hirsch, Poet's Choice, *The Washington Post*

"One of the most exciting writers working in Hebrew today."
  —*Ha'aretz*

REQUIEM

also by AHARON SHABTAI
from New Directions

—

J'accuse
War & Love, Love & War

REQUIEM

Aharon Shabtai

translated by Peter Cole

 A NEW DIRECTIONS BOOK

Published by arrangement with the author

Grateful acknowledgments are made for the epigraphs: from *Collected Poems*, Avraham Ben Yitzhak, translated by Peter Cole, edited and with an afterword by Hannan Hever (Ibis Editions, 2002); and from the *Iliad*, translated by Robert Fitzgerald (Anchor Books, 1975)

Manufactured in the United States of America
First published as New Directions Paperbook 1629 in 2025

Library of Congress Cataloging-in-Publication Data
Names: Shabtai, Aharon, author. | Cole, Peter, 1957– translator.
Title: Requiem / by Aharon Shabtai ; translated by Peter Cole.
Other titles: Reķyiem. English
Description: New York : New Directions Publishing Corporation, 2025.
Identifiers: LCCN 2024056231 | ISBN 9780811239318 (paperback) |
ISBN 9780811239325 (ebook)
Subjects: LCGFT: Poetry.
Classification: LCC PJ5054.S264 R4613 2024 | DDC 892.41/6—dc23/eng/20241214
LC record available at https://lccn.loc.gov/2024056231

10 9 8 7 6 5 4 3 2 1

New Directions Books are published for James Laughlin
by New Directions Publishing Corporation
80 Eighth Avenue, New York 10011

CONTENTS

INTRODUCTION

It's a genealogy of a curious sort. Composed over the past several turbulent years in a pared-down, late style, Aharon Shabtai's *Requiem* shows the poet returning to his literary, ethical, and existential origins—but with a six-decade difference. Readers who already know Shabtai as one of the most provocative and inventive Hebrew poets of the past half century will find in the spareness of this new work radiant traces of his early objectivist mappings, like these from 1973:

in first grade
one learns to write
writing in pencil

one learns to add
one talks and sings of the seasons
of the different

kinds of rain
for the first time in an active way a person encounters a book.

They'll register too the evolution of his poetics through the audacious mock-rabbinic narrative of *Begin*, his unlikely 1986 midrash on names and the Name, concealment and revelation, spun out from two pages of the right-wing former prime minister's autobiography and celebrating his grounded warmth, which the Left, Shabtai felt—*his* Left—had lost. And they'll identify distant echoes of the eruptions of his scandalous *Love*, from two years later ("I'm a man / who murdered love // simply / with his own two hands // took / and snapped its neck / like a lamb"), along with the impulse behind the ferocious and explicitly political, consensus-puncturing poems of the 1990s and 2000s, which offended a good part of Israel's readership when they were published on the pages of the country's leading newspaper.

On display but in recharged ways in *Requiem* is the Shabatian literary line that stretches from the Old Testament prophets to the poets of the Greek Anthology and the Attic dramatists (all of whom Shabtai has brought into a vibrant Hebrew, along with the Homeric epics). Also informing that mix is a Francis Ponge–like absorption of household particulars—one that's alert to the tragicomedy of the human scene and the disarmingly potent meeting of dailiness and binding value.

So it is that between the lines of this collection we hear the poet who during the second Intifada would write of IDF soldiers, in "Rypin"—the title of which refers to the northern-central Polish town his father fled for pre-state Palestine—

> *These creatures in helmets and khakis,*
> *I say to myself, aren't Jews,*
>
> *in the truest sense of the word. A Jew*
> *doesn't dress himself up with weapons like jewelry,*
>
> *doesn't believe in the barrel of a gun aimed at a target,*
> *but in the thumb of the child who was shot at …*

Here, too, is the man who, in "The Reason to Live Here," could diagnose the developing malady when Benjamin Netanyahu first came to power in the 1990s and declare, like Amos and maybe Orpheus—

> *The pure words I suckled from my mother's breasts: Man, Child, Justice,*
> *   Mercy, and so on,*
> *are dispossessed before our eyes, imprisoned in ghettos, murdered at check-*
> *   points.*
>
> *And yet, there's still good reason to stay on and live here—*
> *to hide the surviving words in the kitchen, in the basement, or the bathroom.*

The prophet Melampus saved twin orphaned snakes from the hand of his slaves:
they slithered toward his bed while he slept, then licked the auricles of his ears.

When he woke with a fright, he found he could follow the speech of birds—
so Hebrew delivered will lick the walls of our hearts.

About the barbaric events that unfolded on October 7, 2023, and in their wake the pulverizing of Gaza, Shabtai writes with more sorrow than rage. Well into his eighties now, he works in the folds of the directly objurgatory mode of his previous political poems, but with an uncompromised desire to combat what Abraham Joshua Heschel called—in a book on the biblical prophets—the "coalition of callousness." In a 1944 essay "The Meaning of This War," Heschel wrote of the task of his time: "Tanks and planes cannot redeem humanity ... The killing of snakes will save us for the moment but not forever. The war will outlast the victory of arms if we fail to conquer the infamy of the soul ... The greatest task of our time is to take the souls of men out of the pit." Some three-quarters of a century later, and still considering the Jewish question and the question of Palestine, Shabtai bears witness to

the horror
the calamity
the disgrace,
the rubble of folly
and religion's stupidities,
the dimness of vision
and violence of despair

and knows that none of that will be

repaired by an officer,
a bomb or a plane,
and not by still more blood.

As always, his poems of deep-seated pathos afford startling perspective. The twenty-one lines of "Curriculum Vitae," for instance, describe the arc of a lifetime with chilling economy:

> *When I was born,*
> *the Shoah was just waking up.*
>
> *"Good morning,*
> *chubby little boy,"*
> *she said to me ...*

The poet gets out of bed, years pass, and suddenly darkness is falling:

> *And here*
> *the Shoah is back,*
> *leaning over me, and saying:*
>
> *"Good evening,*
> *learned old man,*
> *enough with the reading—*
> *shut your eyes."*

How is the Shoah back? Is it the slaughter of the al-Aqsa Flood? The corruption and rot of the poet's own society? Its thirst for vengeance in Gaza? All of the above? In the "Parable of the State" we find "Milman, from across the way / on the second floor—" who's said to have died of exhaustion after having killed tens of thousands of flies with a swatter he'd taken off its nail:

> *he crushed them against the wall,*
> *the window panes,*
> *the floor, the shutters,*
> *mounds of them piled up*
> *every day,*
> *and every month—*

However caustic, the mourning here and in so many of these poems is at once precisely directed and somehow general. The loss seems almost total.

Both as a collection and poem by poem, *Requiem* winds back through the upheavals of recent years to acknowledge the spirits of the poet's past and the specter of his own death, which shadows him steadily. The title poem, written in the late summer of 2022, unfurls the most minimal and mythic of plots: A dog is barking all afternoon and keeping the octogenarian poet from napping, or from numbness, calling him, it seems, to join or remember the dead of his Tel Aviv childhood, who suddenly begin to appear before him "strolling / to Hovevei Tzion Street" (and is it coincidental that the street name translates as "Lovers of Zion"—as in the Jewish groups established in the 1880s and '90s, in the wake of Russian pogroms?):

Among the dead
there are plenty
of places to park

on Frug Street.

I go down
and see—across from me—

two cars,

General Avidar's

and a bit to the north

Avramski the contractor's

   and here with
his thin legs
is Gidon Hass,
starting his motorcycle

Auden famously noted that naming poses a test of the critic and also the poet: Does the writer relish the biblical lists of begats, and Homer's catalogue of ships and their officers? Does he savor their textures and structures, their distribution of weight and sound along the line? The surface tension and tonal values that constitute part of their ethical currency? Or does he merely suffer them, or skip them altogether?

"Requiem" embraces the old-world names of people and places as conduits to a cosmos. All are evoked, like the shades of the dead in the *Odyssey*: "Now the souls gathered, stirring out of Erebos, / brides and young men, and men grown old in pain," as Robert Fitzgerald translates Book XI. "Life begins," writes Shabtai in poem 23, "with a siren"

> *in the middle of the night,*
>
> *with all of the neighbors*
> *descending*
>
> *to the shelter*
> *beneath the ground*
>
> *and afterwards climbing*
> *back up and dispersing*
>
> *and then as usual*
> *coming back.*

This, keep in mind, is the 1940s of British Mandatory Palestine, not the 2020s of flattened Gaza and Israel in acute crisis. Again the estranging perspectives of these poems, which reach us less from the arena of struggle than from its margins and the edges of ruin—the death and ruins of cultures, and the individuals who construct and reconstruct them. *Requiem*, in other words, is a book of summonings to recalibrated consciousness—to awareness of lineage and wider relation. The voicings of these poems are Jewish voicings, but in this late-prophetic envisioning, what pertains to one set of voices, and one group of people, holds for all. Shabtai is neither "pro-Israel" nor "pro-Palestine." He is pro-dignity and human integrity, and demonstrates his devotion by disturbing the peace of our language: "Without packing / suitcases / and with no change / of address // as of tomorrow— / I am an emigrant. // I've got an appointment / to apply for a new / passport // and assume its color / will be yellow: / the color of shame."

Translating the elemental force of Shabtai's poems during this monstrous war has provided both sentence and solace: *sentence* because Shabtai confronts us not as what Heschel called a "singing saint" or "moralizing poet," but as "an assaulter of the mind," and with what we regularly prefer not to see. And yet, there is that *solace*, because his poems are powered by a hard-won leverage and fiendish sympathy that give at least this translator hope for all that poetry can still do—in any language, and even in the bleakest dark.

PETER COLE

August 3, 2024

I.

TIKKUN

The horror
the calamity
the disgrace,
the rubble of folly
and religion's stupidities,
the dimness of vision
and violence of despair
won't be repaired by an officer,
a bomb or a plane,
and not by still more blood.
Only wisdom of the heart could mend it
only the surgeon, the doctor,
the good teacher, the teachers
the medic—an Arab, a Jew—
only the quiet traveler
riding a bicycle,
someone carrying a sandwich
and walking along a street,
someone opening their eyes,
someone who speaks with compassion,
someone listening
someone learning and wise
someone waiting and thinking
someone guiding someone
down a path of kindness, affection,
the painter, the poet,
disciples of peace—
only the gardeners of peace.

October 10, 2023

TWO PARABLES

I. PARABLE OF THE STATE

Milman, from across the way
on the second floor—
they say he died of exhaustion
after having killed
thousands and thousands of flies.

He took the fly swatter
off its nail on the wall,
swatted and swatted,
and killed—

in the living room, the kitchen,
the bathroom,
on the microwave,
by day and even at night,
month after month,
year after year

he crushed them against the wall,
the window panes,
the floor, the shutters,
mounds of them piled up
every day,
and every month—

But it wore him out
and he collapsed—
and lay there barely alive,
his head against the wall,
lazy flies
wandering across his bald spot,
and one particularly impudent
large fly
indifferently
picking at his nose.

2. ON THE SITUATION OF THE STATE

Good Benjy—
he of the vigorous gait,
and muscular,
wearing leather gloves
and grasping a dustpan—
killed mice
around the house
for fourteen years,
cleverly, with a smile, persistently
and to a chorus of praise,
until one day, an ordinary morning,
so Kafka relates,
the guy woke
and discovered he had become
an enormous mouse,
larger and heavier than actual mice
and those that he'd killed.
Now he lies in bed,
his feet dangling,
already groomed and powdered
and smiling proudly at all who come
to see him, saying:
"I am the greatest of mice.
There is no other mouse like me!"

February 2024

I'M SAD

I'm sad,
sad, sad
about the dead,
I'm sad about
the dead
about the dead,
about the wounded,
sad
about the homes
sad,
sad, sad
also about the fork
thrown onto the floor,
about the bulbs,
burnt-out and broken
or left behind,
still alive
dangling from the ceiling
in an empty house
with the husks,
with the husks
in the garbage, the sink,
on the mattress . . .

February 2024

CURRICULUM VITAE

When I was born,
the Shoah was just waking up.

"Good morning,
chubby little boy,"
she said to me.

And I got out of bed,
went to kindergarten,
and then to school.

I grew up
and then grew old,
my back is bent,
my eyes have settled on books.
Now darkness is falling
there in the window.

And here
the Shoah is back,
leaning over me, and saying:

"Good evening,
learned old man,
enough with the reading—
shut your eyes."

February 2024

THE EMIGRANT

Without packing
suitcases
and with no change
of address

as of tomorrow—
I am an emigrant.

I've got an appointment
to apply for a new
passport

and assume its color
will be yellow:
the color of shame.

Sadly, I'll slide it out
of its brown envelope.

Friends, as of tomorrow
I'll be a loyal citizen
of the country
of the abducted.

February 2024

PLEASE, DR. FINKELSTEIN

We'll take all the ministers
by the hand, one by one,
and huddle them into a corner
of the kitchen
among the potatoes,
beneath the onions,
while the state itself
we'll transfer, carefully,
in an ambulance
to Ichilov Hospital.
I know a cardiologist,
a world-class specialist,
with wise eyes
and deft hands.
Dear Dr. Finkelstein,
Please, please
roll up your sleeves,
take up your scalpel
and open the state's arteries,
the hardened paths to its heart—
remove the blockages,
so it might brim with truth,
understanding, compassion and sorrow
for all the dead
who harmed not a soul.
Open a window within it
to the future, to change—
so our blood might begin to absorb
the oxygen of peace.

October 7, 2024

II.

REQUIEM

> *Blessed are these,*
> *for they will be gathered to the heart of the world,*
> *wrapped in the mantle of oblivion—*
> *their destiny's offerings unuttered to the end . . .*
>> AVRAHAM BEN YITZHAK, "Blessed Are Those Who Sow"

> *Tell me now, Muses, dwelling on Olympos . . .*
> *who were the Danaän lords and officers?*
>> HOMER, *The Iliad*, Book II

I.

That pain in the neck
dog's been barking
and barking

all afternoon—
my head on the pillow—

to remind me, maybe,
I'm not in myself
but in the world?

Or maybe to keep me
from leaving the dead
behind?

Or else you're calling
from among them

for me to get up
and stand on my feet?

Perhaps as witness
to the fact
that I have no existence,

no trace greater
than that of a pole

or a stone,

a hedgehog or a mouse

being barked at
from the neighbors' garden

2.
My brother's best friend
Barkeh died

Now they're both
strolling
to Hovevei Tzion Street

It's already noon

and at the corner
of Dov Hoz and Frishman

shards of bloody
glass are on

the seat of a car
that crashed

3.
Among the dead
there are plenty
of places to park

on Frug Street

I go down
and see—across from me—

two cars,

General Avidar's

and a bit to the north

Avramski the contractor's

    and here with
his thin legs
is Gidon Hass,
starting his motorcycle

4.
Nothing will change—

our neighbor
Mr. Yaretzky,
the street sweeper,

I'll see in the morning
at the corner of Frishman

and for a moment
he'll die

and then be seen
again with the broom

by the lot
and the two brothers'
vegetable stand

5.
Toward Passover
his widow

Vita

gets to stand
by the sink

a slab of salted
meat between

two kerosene burners:

the blue one and the gray

6.
The orphans
Avram and Shloymeh

in khaki pants
and khaki shorts

are back for the holiday
from Shefayah

and go down into the yard

toward the sprinklers
and lantana bushes

7.
Always,
and even if my eyes are closed,

in the morning
the doors open
to the yard

and the clicking is heard
of the gardener's clippers—
Erich Izrael,

Lotte Kristeller

is guiding the women
on the mats

and every afternoon
going down to the "studio"
from Frishman Street

are Avni and Sternschus

8.
Lucia Shlonsky
won't remember

she threw herself off
the balcony

during the break
I'll go for a walk with her dogs

Billi and Mimi,

and sometimes come evening
at the corner of Dov Hoz

she passes by
with Zechoval

9.
Yaakov always lives
beneath the palm tree

always runs to the balcony
when Barkeh whistles

and on the grass in the dark
they laugh

about
the High Commissioner's balls

10.
If you come up from the sea
to Allenby

along the sidewalk on the left
just after
HaYarkon

at Schiflinger's
kiosk

all afternoon long

Mother's standing there

11.
Mother hates
the kitchen

and now she's happy
to work

selling gum,
soda pop

all afternoon
on Allenby

at Schiflinger's
kiosk

12.
Look,
here's Aharon

coming out
of school

bookbag on
his back

starting to flee
along Frishman
and down Frug

from the twins
Amiram and Giora

13.
There
which is here

we call caca
eh eh

and say
"I need *eh eh*"

and then loudly

"Ima, paper!"
Ima, paper!"

14.
Grandmother's always
calling from

the small balcony toward
the neighbor's balcony:

Mrs. Mark'vitch!
Mrs. Mark'vitch!

Mrs. Mark'vitch!

15.
Father's belt

snaps
again and again

against Aharon's backside.

Come and see:

Father is
made of air,

and even the chair

and the blows are abstract

16.
Whoever doesn't
lend an ear

won't hear

from the bathroom
window:

"Help! Help!

They're killing me!"

17.
The green doors
are open,

in the class
the chairs rest
upside down
on the tables,

at the entrance
a bucket

and at the end
of the empty hall

is Mr. Rosenthal,
the janitor

18.
Without digging
a pit

and spilling the blood
of a black lamb

the door will open
and there will appear

from the dark
stairwell

sheepish, hesitant,

Hanokh Konskevolsky

19.
An Egged bus
painted khaki

has been delayed
in Herzliya.

An hour later
on another bus

advancing between
cypresses breaking
up the rays

of the sun
from the west

we'll reach Rishpon

20.
Shalom, shalom!

In a line
along the ridge

against the backdrop of twilight

above Yotvata

coming out of
Baruchaleh's wedding

the older people are waving at us:

Shalom, shalom!

21.
The broom
like a thin,

modest man

and tall—
close as a brother,

leans against the wall
in the hallway

quiet and ready
at the entrance to the kitchen

22.
Aharon,
a mediocre student,

is going to study
at the kibbutz;

the dead know
he'll go far

very far

and then
return

23.
Life begins
with a siren

in the middle of the night,

with all of the neighbors
descending

to the shelter
beneath the ground

and afterwards climbing
back up and dispersing

and then as usual
coming back

24.
Grandmother
doesn't use
newspaper

in a corner
of the kitchen
on the waxed tabletop

she smooths out
and patiently collects

pieces of thin
tissue in which
oranges were packed

25.
A knock on the door,
who is it?

It's Mr. Beigel

with a package
of starched shirts
and sheets.

And the rest—

towels, underwear,
pants, socks—

we take in a sack
and pass on to Hamilevski
at the corner
of Yisraelis Street

26.
When Yaakov returns
he jokes around
with Grandmother:

*"Frau Pomerantz
(or "Pomenyu")*

*zol ikh hubn
gite teg*

*und
gite nekht*

vi di ost!"

27.
Aharon doesn't have friends
in kindergarten

they're only in the kitchen,
in the upper drawer:

the hammer,
the "Gamal Pascha" screwdriver,
the "Killer" pliers

and in the drawer for silverware

is an old and fancy fork
with swirls like Ben
Gurion's hair

28.
And Ahareleh
(Prokopetz)

from the family
of vegetarians

who left a yellow
stain of poop

next to Yivarkhayhu's
bike

chained to a pipe

next to the entrance

29.
Camels loaded with sand
pass
on King George

in the shack across from them
Aunt Hava

at the entrance
over the step

is peeling carrots

and in the window
next to the roller

is Hirsch Leib

30.
The co-op's run

by Solganik (the manager),
by Hannah and by Tzitron,

at the counter by the register

in front of the wide window

sits Freida

and Mother's collecting
money for Adam,
the new worker

31.
Father's going
with me

to Mr. Neiberg,

his legs are swollen,

he won't go back

to construction

Nearby, on Dizengoff,
north of Gordon
in a ground-floor apartment,
lives Brontcha

32.
Hannah Raskin's
kindergarten

has a yard,
a place to play,

and in the back room

there's a picture of her husband
who drowned at sea,

and on the floor above
on the balcony

you can see
Tanhum Cohen Mintz

33.
Most beautiful of all
on Lesbos
is Anactoria,

and in class—

Ilana Lustgarten's
face

Shoshana Fuchs's
eyes,

Sarah Aloni's
legs

34.
Tami Eshkol gave
Aharon a slap

Mrs. Mandelblatt
shouts from the window

toward the grass

Grandmother's crossing
Dov Hoz

and going up to
Mrs. Tchernemorsky

35.
From the far entrance
across from us

Dov Shtock emerges

In the afternoon Mr. Sapir
parks his bread cart

ties a bag of grain
to the horse's head

and stocky Mr. Yablonsky
marches along

throwing his legs
right and left

Mother calls it:
"*Hoopche deroopche*"

36.
A little Eden

is the bench in the garden
of the health clinic

on the corner of Mendele

with Drs. Levova
and Forshener,
the vigorous Nurse Krasnova

and, in case of emergency,
there is no better
and kinder
physician to call

than Dr. Gottlieb

37.
You enter through
the nurse's room

and place your bruised knee

in the soft leather saddle
(which is lowered and raised)

on a stand made of white
tubing and a round base,

and here's the orange iodine
and like a cross

white or brown
Band-Aids

38.
But along the way
at the corner of Dov Hoz

be sure to stop
at the shoemaker's stall

and give him a shoe to repair
with his hammer and nails

but take care
(if you're passing anywhere near)

not to run

into his middle child
Moyshe Zelman

39.
Or pass by and go on
and cross
Mendele

to the island
with the two trees

and the two benches
set
back to back

and you'll see opposite you

Rafi Kaufman's father,

punctual,
with straw-colored hair,

getting out of his
green Henry J

40.
Amnon Weinstein,
in love,

is wandering around beneath
Ilana Shiffman's

balcony.

In the lot
between Kassit and Roval
while pouncing after a ball

a wound wide as a mouth
was opened in his knee

by a shard
from a green bottle

41.
And here
all dolled up

and coming out of her

parent's apartment

is Penina Zaltzman.

"He's screwing my daughter!"
Mr. Shmueli shouts

(running after
Yoram Raskin)

down the street

42.
Yoel's born,

Yaakov and I are lying
in the lower bunk

head to foot.

I didn't hear Father
screwing Mother

not even from
the bed

in the next room

43.
In the black cupboard

hidden behind
rows of books
with the green and blue covers

of Stiebel and Mitzpeh editions,

sits, tattered:

Human Sex Life

(by
Dr. A. Matmon)

44.
Have a look

at *Gauguin*
(by André Maurois)

and you can see
on a smooth page

actual
naked breasts

45.
Mother's recommending
Balzac

and sending me
to Lahover

the librarian
at Beit Brenner

(the 5 bus
to Shenkin Street)

I also borrow

from the North Library—
and also from Lauterbach

46.
Less rewarding
is the barbershop

with
the green cushions
(the armrests)

near
the corner of Frishman.

It's better to go
by the Square

to Muzikant

and not to get your hair cut
by his brother
or anyone else,

only him

47.
"Ach, if only I had something to give him!"
Mother says

when,
under the swaying model planes

on the bedspread
by my elbow

a book is open:
The Life of Beethoven

48.
Unlike me,
Uzi Weinberg
borrows books

from Phela
at the Hymnon,

whereas

in the bathroom
we would sit
and masturbate together

49.
Under the heavy blanket,
as though in a submarine,

embracing one
or a pair of girls

at night you'll navigate
far and into the depths

down down

and suddenly in the dark
on the sheet

the white liquid
pools

50.
Shmulik
Sheinberg's father

makes floor tiles,

Uzi's father,
Elimelekh,
has an oil tanker

and a gas station,

and my father's in love
with Ta'ira's legs

51.
Even though he died
with his wife

after a pesticide leak
from the neighbor's apartment,

Solganick
isn't likely to forget

to leave my mother

two bottles
of dark malt

in the hall
beside the door

to the storage room

52.
Chen Barsky
grows up facing
the margosa tree

his red-faced father
manages the "Argaz,"

his mother gets
meat from me
wrapped in a newspaper

she opens a door
and the light goes on
inside the Crosley fridge

53.
The door to Mrs. Markovitz's
was locked

and Hasson,
the son of Nehamaleh's

piano teacher,

is climbing from the balcony

to the balcony
on the third floor

and opening up from within

54.
Come evening,
across from Kristeller's charges
on the mats

in the hall
open to the yard

even the trees
and the bushes

are envious of Yaakov who's standing
with pretty Tamar

from
Kibbutz Ayn HaHoresh

55.
Father fell from the scaffolding

his leg
was put in a cast
in the back of a van

and covered with towels,

and on Friday
as though on the sly

Yosolov
the sad-sack worker

brings some pigeons

56.
Father happily joins
Carmi the architect

going from floor to floor

on the wooden planks
nailed to the pitch
of the concrete

there isn't much in the way
of competition

maybe Toib,

he's happy with
a local foreman

in Holon,
Yitzhak Eisenstat

57.
Father's brought in
this time
with a broken finger

from a heavy hammer.

At the Histadrut
headquarters

he looks out over the wing

standing on the railing
of the third or fourth floor,

and down at the administrators' hut
are Weissman and Zuckerman

58.
Like Plutarch
I have to mention

long, silent, ruddy Yulish
gripping the large saw

which he'd taken from the sack,

and Tzitron
and Shmuel Leiter

angels of the concrete casting

it's only too bad that Tzitron laughs
when the tomato juice spritzes

from Yaakov Schiflinger's
mouth while he's eating

59.
In Rishpon
the bus stops

by Uncle Tzadok's
house

Aunt Rahel
chops vegetables

on the table
by the dairy

Rex, the dog,
sprawls on the porch

60.
At night,
by oil lamp

we go into the dark

to a hut,
an outhouse

the poop hits
the bottom of the pit

By day
the guys come
for Sarah and Tzilah

and crack up:

"We went to the dairy,
Plop, plop plop ..."

61.
At the edge of the moshav—
Aunt Malka,

and Uncle Nahman

who took from a drawer

a red sharpener made of Bakelite
for me

on upper Allenby
one evening

in the office
of "The Contractors' Center"

62.
Father's helping him
build

the brooder coop

His daughter Avivit
who served in Egypt

during the days
of Al-Alamein

is visiting with Edwin,
who's tall

and wears the blue suit and tie
of Maccabi Cairo

63.
The homes are all in a row,

and attached to every house
by a long chain
a dog is barking

In the last house

are Aunt Carmela,
Ephraim, their son Yaakov
and Granny Gila

There too
the oil lamp lights the way

as you step
through the dark along the path

to the hut
of an outhouse

64.
"Make me a cup of tea
with nails"—

Uncle Tzadok half asleep
would mutter in Yiddish

And what does Uncle Nahman
have to say?

"My son's flying
aeroplanes!"

65.
Across the road
in Arsoof

Eizikov's
milking a cow

across from that
next to Gutcha
and Rabby's house

Yoel Konskevolsky
is parking a yellow
D2 tractor

He's short and has
a flat nose

and recently came
back from Abadan

66.
The park is empty

only Yehudit
is on the grass

Mother
is pushing a cart

All of Meir Park—

the grass, the bushes,
the branches—

grows from Yehudit's
quiet, lazy hair

67.
From time to time
Anja comes

to Ita Poznansky
on Ranak Street

opposite the Ma'avir
parking lot.

And on Shabbat
in Itzik's truck

we travel to Magdiel.

Shmulik, the son, is in bed
in the picture

but was sent
to a kibbutz

68.
There's a little joy,
not much,

in the ration of

the fresh bread's "kiss,"
two cubes of chocolate.

The house lets people in—

Tzvi Nordenberg
Motek Furman,

and lets them out—
Rozengarten

69.
Everything's in place
coming and going
in people's hands

at the door

Kachuli takes
Flames in Ash from a suitcase

and sells it to Mother

with books of poems
by Yitzhak Katznelson

70.
Early one morning

the sound of kisses
is heard in the hall

kisses
with the taste of sweat

from the cheeks
of Yaakov Schiflinger
(Mother's cousin)

a concentration
camp alum

who was suddenly
released from Cyprus

71.
His brother Abrasha
is still in Mannheim

he's making money

and sports golden rings
on a hairy hand,

he'll get married
and send Yoel a piano

72.
A drop of blood

is left on the tile
by the British soldier

wearing the
red beret
who was scratched when they came

in to take
Father and Mother

to the lockup
during the Great Curfew

(they stole a tin of Father's stamps
from the cupboard)

and today we'll stay
with Grandmother

73.
The children run around
on the roof

throwing
water bombs,

onto the garden center
at the corner
of Frishman and Dizengoff

armored cars are parked

and you can hear
the soldiers' bagpipes

74.
(the Scotsmen's).

And in the dark
at the corner of Dov Hoz

next to the barbed-
wire checkpoint

they stop you and ask:

"Are you
from the Stern Gang?"

75.
Isma', Isma'

Mother calls
from the porch

to the Arab kids
who are shouting: *Sardines!*

Below
by the entrance

the hand is raised
holding a stick

and the fish
are weighed on scales

76.
Fresh turds
fall on the road

toward noon

On the asphalt
are rows of droppings

Hayyim up front—
a thin piece of paper between his lips—
is holding the sharp pick

and stops the wagon
covered with tin:

"Aharon, get off,
bring the ice"

77.
Five or six steps
below ground

on Dov Hoz Street
as though from Hades

Aryeh Pozner
the plumber climbs
up from the storage room's dark

to lift off a cover
and open up
a blocked sewer pipe

across from the hibiscus

next to Khruvi's
balcony

78.
"Discuses"
we all called

Mother's cakes
as they came out of the oven

but here to save
the day is

Mrs. Klopman

with five
normal cakes

and they're in the bathtub
waiting for Shabbat and the bar mitzvah

79.
At Rabbi Grossman's
house

next to Synagogue
Beit El

one can hear
Haftorah study:

"And again David assembled ..."

How beautiful the rabbi's granddaughter is
passing by

and time after time
Nahumi the beadle appears

80.
I'm still on Haya Pozner's balcony

on Reines Street

Joseph is ill
and won't return to construction,

the cake was eaten

it's sad after Shabbat:
there's school tomorrow

81.
There were two good years
in fourth and fifth grade

with Devorah Weber,

Yaakov was still there in the third

He's accompanied
from the long-jump pit

by Mrs. Polturak, the teacher

patting him on the back

82.
Everything's repeated:

"Listen, rain ..."
the song goes—

and Yoram Murkes

and at recess
Miss Aharoni
going outside

to the teachers'
bathroom

And the tip
of Orah Sandhaus's
raised finger

always bent
a little backwards

83.
And here's a new teacher,
with tree-trunk legs:

Dr. Finkelbrand.

Aharon's sent to sit
by Feller's office,

and in seventh grade
it's possible to talk

about Tolstoy at recess

with the teacher
Tamar Dolzhansky

84.
"I read a lot too!"

says
Dalia Schwartz,

whose father is
a tax collector

Ori Rabinovitz's
mother

has an electric
vacuum cleaner

and Ephraim Yaffe's father

face flushed
and wearing a leather hat

arrives on his motorcycle

85.
The neighbor
Mrs. Rosengarten

opens the door
in her underwear

it's hot in summer,
her legs are the color of milk

she comes in
and bursts out laughing:

"Yankele! Yankele!"

86.
From the window
of the outhouse

you can see the beginning
of Mapu Street

and opposite—
Amos Lev's apartment

Tzurik's apartment

and below
Kretchmer's balcony

near
the garbage shed

87.
The quarrels stopped

over keeping
the outhouse clean—

Yaakov Vilensky

enlisted in
the Brigade—

Miriam and Ehud
take the small
room for rent

and on the balcony
in a crate

sits an electric hotplate

88.
From Miriam's mouth
in the small room
one hears
for the first time:

"Fries"

On the way from WIZO

in netlike bags she'd bring—
from the British dispensary,
the NAAFI—

packages of biscuits
and waffles

and cans of sardines

89.
From the radio
we hear:

"*The British police,*
Chichchika booooom

Ay ay this isn't good …"

And in the shower
Miriam sings

"Habibi,
everything passes, habibi ..."

90.
Across from the Mizrahi Girls School
in the park,
during a class gathering
one evening

on the bench

are revealed
beneath skirts

the two
pure white backsides

of Ruti and Nili
Kartun

91.
Mossi Badler
died of leukemia

after his mother—

a redhead,
his short khaki pants
get stuck in his crack

as he runs
around playing games
in the yard

His father,
active in Mapam,

doesn't forget to wave
the red flag

92.
Below,
on the second floor

Ziv Sukher
who died
on one mission or another

and on the first floor
Yosi Lippa

who won't pass by anymore
barefoot

near the co-op

93.
In the wing beside it,
on the third floor
under the roof

one door next to another—

Hayim Glasberg
("Kutchu")

his father rides
a bike

with clothespins
at the hem of his pants

and Ilan Spivak

94.
His sister—Drora

draws
the boys to her

whereas Aviva

Nehameleh's sister

is taller

and has a birthmark
on her leg

95.
I'm shifted to
a foldout bed

in Grandmother's room

Before I fall asleep

Grandpa Beier
undresses

and leaves
on the floor

a large,
clumsy hernia belt

like
a horse's harness

96.
Miriam
pulls an almost

transparent minnow

out from the rocks
at Frishman Beach

and on the sand

we learn
from Nehameleh's father

that a cucumber
is eaten

with its
green skin

97.
Tzurik's still singing:

*"Who is that
who in the kitchen*

*left behind
his mind?"*

But Pinhas
and Aviezer Ripin

went out into life,

they no longer go down
to the yard

to build the *sukkah*

98.
Tziona Shimshi
in a blue blouse

is chattering away on the corner
by the fence
with Dana and Nira

Come evening
by flashlight
on the road

they dance

and through the shutters
I hear:

*"Who's there
wandering around*

among the trees ..."

99.
Austerity—

a prix-fixe lunch at Kassit
near Shlonsky

costs
38 cents

Or
on the way to the square
in front of the restaurant

on the sidewalk
the swarthy Mrs. Haan

announces to the kitchen:

*"Zwei
hoppel poppel!"*

100.
There is no May
Day parade

without Barkeh
leading the drummers

The bike brigade
is at the back
with its decorated
spokes and wheels

and always on the side
along Dizengoff
walks

Yankele Tikulsky
(later Agmon)

101.
So long little shack—

Mahanot ha-Olim
(with *"Jim Malaya!"*

and hand to hand
combat training).

So long, Munjak,
our troop leader!

Aharon's now
in Shomer HaTza'ir
(at the Central "Nest")

among the beautiful girls
(Maya and Nili Sela)

and hears the command
"Eyes front!"

from Ori Dvir

102.
How beautifully
the brigade leader speaks—
Eve Taub,

it hurt
to see her

in the arms of someone else

facing the sea

their backs to the tombstones
of the Muslim graveyard

103.
At the Nest,
Buma's lecturing
on the Kolkhoz,

while outside

two redheads
are dribbling

Yosi and Moishe
(Yonji and Monji)

and the shooters run
from basket to basket

Pini, and "Kakkao"

(Yisrael Paz's
brother)

104.
We sing
Russian songs

"Wide and mighty,

O Dnipro, Dnipro ..."

And at home
Father tears
pictures of Stalin

down from the clothes closet

105.
The Torch tribe
leaders are changing:

Shaykeh and
Uri Selah,

instead of
swarthy Me'ira.

Her boyfriend—Hatzkul

goes down
to the Shevakh School

at the Silicate lot

holding
a bottle of milk

106.
We won't forget
Dantchik

Yitzhakeleh,

Marit,

Breitzeleh,

Amnon Avukay,

Yehudah Shevek

And also
Maitel

107.
It's evening at the Nest

Yaakov

takes me aside

and by the fence

shows me
a thin young man,

sickly,
acned, short,

"Here,
meet Maitel"

108.
Everyone marches
in threes

on Bograshov

up
toward the sea

passing the square

(Hanokh once
lived there)

making the short
walk between
the Eucalyptus trees

and the Moriah School

109.
Mother's still
young

and carries
baskets of food

from the shops
on her bike

"Masha,
Why don't you
come around more often?"

the poet Rahel asks

on HaYarkon Street

110.
At the Shalvah court

go and you'll
get a ball

from Tzvi Katcherginsky

on someone's shoulders
Jemel

hangs the nets

this time Israel
Paz is the ref

and for a few minutes
the coaches play:

Micha Shamban
and Barukh Schlein

III.
Skinny Yair Hurvitz
is sitting

on the small booth
looking out

over the jute sheets
tied to the fence

toward the Maccabee
basketball court.

Who'll win
the Magen Amiram
championship game—

Avraham Shneor

or David Heiblum?

112.
And who's the fairest
woman of all?

Rochel Cohen?

Helah,
Barkeh's mother?

Kushi's wife
(Tziporah Leiter's
sister),

Itta Falevitz?

113.
That pain in the neck
dog is barking
and barking,

the day deepens
and stretches out,
turning—into eternity.

Don't wait
for Heracles to come

Bark

bark with us

bark for all of us—

the living dead

on Frug Street

October 2022

III.

THE QUIET

In the end, the end,
thanks, and the quiet come
in place of the noise,
all that chatter
rolling around
in mounds in the room,
in the road, on the sidewalk,
the computer screen.
In front of the chair,
on the bed,
by a faucet,
mouth shut
and breath alone saying:
"So long, won't be in touch . . ."

October 2022

FROM "AHARON"

DEATH

Now death
is waiting for Aharon

others aren't waiting

Death wants him

not in so many words
but as a fact

And Aharon's fine with that
and so is Death

which wants nothing
but to be
Aharon to Aharon

AHARON

I'm Aharon
and have a friend,
and he's Aharon

Aharon's straight with me,
he lies beside me
and doesn't leave

He doesn't add anything to me
or take anything away

Aharon plus Aharon
equals Aharon

Aharon minus Aharon
equals Aharon

And when Aharon's lonely
here comes Aharon

and when Aharon dies
so will Aharon

OBLIVION

Aharon isn't
forgotten yet

he's lying quietly
in oblivion

but there's a certain someone
in a certain place
on a certain day

reading a poem
by Aharon

about a bed in which
people are forgotten

and about a glass
in the kitchen

which is empty

then filled with water

then empty again

THE END

Aharon comes
Aharon goes

Life was good—
always sandals, always shoes

Aharon thanks
the sandals and shoes

Love is good
without a doubt

although the end
has to come

and even a bad
end is a good one

FEAR

Sometimes when Aharon's
reflected to Aharon

through the half dark
in a closet mirror

Aharon says,
looking at Aharon:

"It's you I'm afraid of,

you who are
so close to me

and are so slowly
being given

over to me—
that's what's killing me"

DESCENT

Aharon's flying as usual
but downwards
rather than up

and everything
is as it was
in the same direction

at the same angle
in front of our faces,

the cauliflower in the refrigerator
and the bed

and the cognac in the flask
is good on the way up
and not bad going down

HAPPY

Aharon's down
but still happy,

that's his nature,

he's a person
who's made for happiness

like the darkness
that covers a tomato

all the darkness in the world
covers a tomato

and the tomato's in the dark

but the darkness is darkness
and the tomato a tomato

POEMS COME

Poems come
with thinking

like blood pulsing
through Aharon's heart

He sends them on
from speech to silence,

he lets them go,
so they won't be poems

so they'll pass
by and be forgotten

when he wants to
lie down and rest

BALANCE

A balance exists,
and Aharon's place
is taken by Aharon

When it's good for Aharon
he doesn't write

He just lives

And when it's bad for Aharon,
when there is no love
and the body's weak and aching,

he prepares for death

Aharon will vanish
and there will be
only Aharon's poems

April 2015

BIOGRAPHICAL NOTES

AHARON SHABTAI was born in 1939 in Tel Aviv and grew up there and on Kibbutz Merhavia. The author of twenty-three volumes of poetry, he is also the foremost translator of ancient Greek literature into Hebrew, having published over thirty plays in annotated editions, as well as both the *Iliad* and the *Odyssey*. Three previous selections of his work have appeared in English translations by Peter Cole: *Love & Selected Poems* (Sheep Meadow Press, 1997), *J'accuse* (New Directions, 2003), which received the PEN Prize for Poetry in Translation, and *War & Love, Love & War: Selected Poems* (New Directions, 2010).

PETER COLE is the author of six books of poems—most recently *Draw Me After* (FSG, 2022)—and has translated widely from Hebrew and Arabic literature, medieval and modern. He has received numerous honors for his work, including a PEN Translation Prize, a Guggenheim Foundation Fellowship, a MacArthur Fellowship, and an American Academy of Arts and Letters Award in Literature.